Trick Your Dog into Obedience

By

Nancy Milburn

Foreword

Traditionally, dog training has been seen as a power struggle. The concept of the 'alpha dog' having to be the boss, or top dog, influenced peoples approach to training. This often meant harsh treatment while training and corrections were given with pain generating equipment.

The concept of teaching obedience in the same manner as teaching a trick is revolutionary. Training is achieved gently and surprisingly quickly.

Trick training can easily be done at home BUT remember that socialization is also a very important part of dog training. Please make sure your dog is friendly with all other animals big and small and all humans too.

Your dog is unemployed and looking for work! Give your dog lots to do and you will build a relationship that will bring pleasure to both of you for years.

History of Dog Training

Traditional obedience training methods tend to be boring, for both dog and handler. Endless repetitions of sit, down, stay etc. mean that a great deal of determination is necessary to complete the course and have a well trained dog.   Long before there were puppy classes and obedience schools, people trained their dogs at home using the reward method, meaning when the dog obeyed a command they got something tasty to eat. Also, the training would be done in short bursts, instead of an hour at a time.

Almost all dog training methods work. This is because they use forms of classical conditioning. In simple terms this is where the dog does something and one of three things happen:

- There is no result (the handler ignores the dog)
- There is a positive result (the handler gives food, praise and /or play time,)
- There is a negative result (the dog experiences pain or discomfort) the handler uses choke chain, prong collar or jerks the leash.

During the Second World War the German shepherd was used by the German Army. These well trained dogs impressed the Allied forces with their courage under fire and the commands that they obeyed. These dogs had been trained under harsh army conditions with choke chains and negative conditioning. Consequently when the soldiers brought back stories of these marvellous dogs, the harsh military training methods became the mainstream way of obedience training for ordinary pets. Some dog schools went as far as to use the German words for the commands i.e. platz instead of lie down.

Choke chains became the norm, even for the smallest dogs, although not everyone was using them correctly. They must be worn in such a way that they release easily, and only used with a short, sharp jerk to gain the dog's attention, and then quickly released. When used incorrectly, the chain will choke the dog, cause great distress and may permanently damage the trachea. Some dogs will pull on the leash keeping the choke chain tight around their neck, thus neutralizing the training effects of this tool.

When I began to teach dog obedience, choke chains were the tools of choice. But I found that there were some people who used it as a punishment instead of an attention getting there was also some who were uncomfortable with the concept of the choke chain, feeling that they would not like to hurt their dog in any way. This made teaching somewhat frustrating. So I stopped using choke chains for training and all dogs were to wear leather or nylon collars. This was a great improvement, but there were still handlers who used the leash and collar to reprimand their dogs. This is when I started training obedience like a trick.

When obedience commands are learned like tricks, training is simple and easy because with no harsh treatment, the dogs enjoy learning and are not afraid to make mistakes. If they do something incorrectly then there is no reward but also no punishment.

When teaching a trick, if the dog does not respond you do not discipline the dog, you just try again, maybe doing something a little different. When you get the correct or partially correct response, praise the dog in a bright happy voice and give a food reward.

Trick training is so easy that even young children can learn to easily control small or large dogs. But it is always best to always keep dogs and children under supervision at all times. Even the best trained dog can be distracted. Training should be carried out in a safe enclosed area.

An easy way to help with distractions is for the dog to wear a collar with a six foot or longer leash attached. You can stand on the leash near the end and the dog is prevented from leaving, but still will not receive any leash corrections.

This book was written for those people who want to have a well trained dog, but also one that is fun to have around. Happy Training!!

How and Why Trick Training Works

- IT'S FUN!
- Positive interaction between you and your dog
- Dogs like to have a job. With some breeds it is absolutely essential
- All dogs have a natural instinct to find food – you can use this to your advantage
- Rewarding a simple action with food trains your dog simply and easily as you are utilizing a very strong motivator
- Traditional dog training tends to be boring for the dog, endless repetition with little or now reward, sometimes using pain as a corrective tool. This only creates fear in your dog. A happy dog is more responsive
- When trick training, the trainer never corrects, only ignores an incorrect response. This means the dog is not afraid to make mistakes.

Before you start

- When interacting with your dog NEVER be angry or bark orders
- Happy tones or baby talk works best
- Trick training is fun. Make sure your dog is having fun
- His tail (if he has one) should be wagging happily
- Go slowly – do not overwhelm your dog
- Make sure the first trick you teach your dogs is to take rewards gently

Age

Training should start as soon as your dog comes home with you or as soon as you have finished reading this book! Your dog will be watching you all the time looking for clues:

Are you getting his food?

Are you going out?

Are you getting ready to take him out?

These are just a few examples of what he is trying to work out. It is never too late to start training – older dogs may take more time to achieve results but perseverance will eventually work

Breed

All breeds benefit from training. All breeds can learn tricks. The number of tricks depends on how dedicated you are as the trainer. Even the so called 'hared to train' dogs can be easily trained by this method.

Rewards

With trick training you must have rewards that your dog enjoys. Combinations of food, toys and your excitement work best. Typical food rewards include liver, cheese, dog biscuits, wieners (caution – some dogs are sensitive to additives and/or colour is some commercially produced foods)

Jackpots – Special Rewards

Always praise your dog enthusiastically but when he completes a trick correctly for the first time, go overboard with a bigger treat, tons of praise – jump up and sown and hug your dog, say hooray or whoopee! The more excited you are the more your dog will try and so well the next time you ask for a trick.

Places to train

- Begin by training in a place familiar to both you and your dog, either inside your home or a fenced back yard
- When your dog does what you ask in your home gradually include other familiar places, either relatives homes or familiar walks
- Treat areas you walk or train your dog responsibly and always take care around strangers

Equipment

- Rewards/Lures – food or toys
- Leather of fabric collar and/or regular harness
- 6' leash

Most teaching is done without any equipment except rewards. Collars, leashes and harnesses are used only during learning the process to prevent your dog from leaving your side

Equipment *not* to use

- Head halters, choke chains, prong collars, slip collars, martingale collars, chain leashes or long lines made of wire

What is a Nose Magnet?

- When you find a reward your dog likes, use it as a nose magnet
- Lure your dog by keeping the reward no more than 1" from your dog's nose
- Always move the nose magnet very slowly when training something new

How to use this book

- I recommend that you read all the information before you start with the tricks
- Go slow while progressing – make sure all signals are slow and exaggerated in the beginning
- Read each trick thoroughly before starting to teach the trick
- Always start with 'Look at Me' and follow the trick in the order stated
- I recommend learning the tricks in the order listed
- Always review tricks your dog already knows before staring new tricks
- Always finish each session with an easy trick your dog can do i.e. 'Sit'
- Advanced tricks can only be taught if basic ones are known first. Any trick that you need to know first will be underlined   HAVE FUN!

Tricks

Gentle

Your dog takes food gently from you hand. Your dog needs to learn this before going on tho other tricks

- Hold reward in your hand with only a small amount showing
- Offer the reward to your dog
- Say 'Gentle'
- Release reward only if your dog **slowly** comes toward the reward
- If dog rushes toward your hand or bites your hand, say 'Gentle' loudly but do not let reward go
- Do not remove you hand from near your dog's mouth but say 'Gentle' again – only let the reward go once your dog takes it gently

Look at Me

Used to gain your dogs attention

- Trainer stands upright
- Hold reward in from of your nose
- Say your dog's name
- Give reward and say 'Look at Me' as your dog looks at you
- If you dog does not look at you, put the reward to his nose and say 'Look at Me' as you bring the reward up to your nose
- Repeat – stand upright
- Say 'Look at Me' holding treat in front of your nose
- Count 2 seconds
- Give reward
- Repeat adding 2 seconds each time until you hold your dog's attention for 20 seconds
- Jackpot

Sit

- Say '<u>Look at Me</u>'
- Hold reward just above your dog's nose
- Move reward over the back of your dog's head so that his neck is stretched upwards with his nose pointing to the ceiling
- Your dog will automatically 'Sit'
- As soon as his bottom touches the floor say 'Sit' and give reward
- Say 'Sit' and hold the reward to lure him to 'Sit'
- Take a step away from your dog to make him stand
- Give reward as soon as his bottom touches the floor
- Now work up to 15 seconds between saying 'Sit' and giving reward
- Jackpot

Down

- Say 'Look at Me'
- Say 'Sit'
- Hold reward just in front of your dog's nose
- Say 'Down' slowly dropping your hand to the floor. Keep your dog's nose not ore that 1" from reward luring him 'Down'
- As soon as he is on the floor say 'Down' and give reward
- Now build up to 15 seconds between saying 'Down' and him remaining in the 'Down; position – give reward
- Jackpot

Stand

Your dog stands without moving

- Say '<u>Look at Me</u>'
- Say '<u>Sit</u>'
- Hold reward just in front of your dog's nose
- Slowly draw the reward forward until your dog has to take a step
- Say 'Stand' and give reward
- Practice the 'Stand' until he can stand without moving for 15 seconds
- Also practice 'Stand' from the 'Down' position
- Once your dog is '<u>Down</u>' use the reward as a nose magnet bringing it up at a45 degree angle
- Jackpot

Bow

Your dog's front end goes down and he holds this position for a moment

- Say '<u>Look at Me</u>'
- Say 'Stand'
- Hold reward in front of your dog's nose
- Lure front end of your dog down quickly with a reward until his elbows are on the floor
- The reward should be near your dog's chest between his front legs to lure his nose down
- Rear legs should stay standing
- Say 'Bow' and give reward
- Jackpot

Push-ups

Your dog changes position from stand to down several times

- With your dog in a standing position say '<u>Down</u>' – making sure your dogs goes straight down and does not sit first
- Reward one your dog is down
- From the down position say '<u>Stand</u>' again. Make sure your dog does not sit between down and stand
- Say 'Push-ups' and repeat gradually getting faster
- Reduce number of rewards until your dog will do several 'Push-ups for one reward

Roll Over

From a down position your dog rolls 360 degrees onto his back and continues the roll into the down position

- Say 'Look at Me'
- Say 'Down'
- All of his legs must be on the same side as his nose
- Hold reward in front of your dog's nose
- SLOWLY make your dog's head point toward his rear legs and continue moving the reward over his shoulder
- As his nose is slowly drawn over his shoulder he will naturally twist his body to follow the reward
- As he completes the roll over give reward saying 'Roll Over'
- Jackpot

Roll Back

Once your dog has mastered 'Roll Over' reverse the procedure and say 'Roll Back'
Jackpot

Caution – Very large, old or overweight dogs might not be able to manage this trick

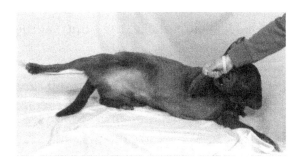

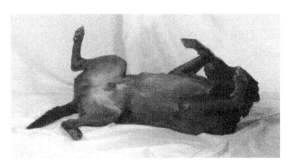

Paw

Your dog lifts his paw and allows you to hold it

- Say 'Look at Me'
- Say 'Sit'
- Hold reward in your right hand
- With your left hand gently tap your dog's right front leg behind 1st joint
- As your dog lifts his leg, hold it and say 'Right Paw'
- Reverse procedure for the 'Left Paw'
- Be consistent with 'Left Paw' or 'Right Paw' always tap correct paw and your dog will learn the difference
- Jackpot

High-Five

Your dog sits and raises one paw to touch the palm of your hand

- Say 'Look at Me'
- Say 'Sit'
- Say 'Paw' – reward
- Repeat
- Ask your dog to 'High-five'
- Have your palm facing the dog with your fingers pointing upwards letting your dog touch your palm
- Give reward
- Start with your hand low to the ground and each time you ask for 'High-Five' lift your hand higher and higher
- Jackpot

Wave Hello

Your dog sits and lifts on paw up to his face level and waves his paw

- Say 'Look at Me'
- Say 'Sit'
- Say 'Paw'
- Say 'High-Five' 3 times reward each time
- Give the 'Wave Hello' hand signal and say 'Wave Hello'. Do not let his paw touch your palm – give reward
- Stand one step away from your sitting dog – way 'Wave Hello' and give hand signal
- Reward for any movement of paw off the ground
- Continue with verbal command and hand signal rewarding for higher and higher paw movements
- Jackpot

Repeat these hand signals for 'Wave Hello'

Sit Pretty

Your dog sits on his hind legs and lifts his front legs off the ground

- Say '<u>Look at Me</u>'
- Say '<u>Sit</u>'
- Hold reward just above your dog's nose lifting it up slowly towards your dog's back
- Very slowly make your dog stretch his head toward the ceiling
- Your dog will slowly let his front feet come off the ground
- As his feet leave the ground say 'Sit Pretty' and give reward
- Gradually increase the distance his front legs come off the ground saying 'Sit Pretty' and giving reward
- Jackpot

Caution – Very large, long backed, old or overweight dogs might not be able to manage this trick

Off – Take it

Your dog removes his paws or mouth from whatever they are touching
Your dog only takes something on command

- Say 'Look at Me'
- Hold a reward in your fingers close to your dog's nose
- As your dog's mouth touches your fingers to take the reward say 'Off' quite loudly, bumping your dog's nose gently if necessary, to make him back off
- After your dog has backed off say 'Take it' and give him the reward
- Repeat increasing the number of seconds between saying 'Off' and 'Take it' until you get to 15 seconds

Go Pee

Your dog urinates on command

- Take your dog on his leash to pee are
- Wait for your dog to pee
- Say 'Go Pee' as your dog is peeing
- Reward within 3 seconds of your dog finishing
- Repetition of this will encourage your dog to pee in the same spot

Go Poop

Your dog defecates on command

- Take your dogs on his leash to a poop area
- Wait for dog to poop
- Say 'Go Poop' as your dog poops
- Reward within 3 seconds of your dog finishing
- Repetition of this will encourage your dog to always use the same spot

Alternate words are 'Go Potty', Hurry Up' or 'Do your Business'

Paws Up

Your dog stands on his hind legs and puts his front paws on the object indicated

- Show the reward to your dog
- Place reward on chair, counter or bed
- Say 'Paws Up' and tap the reward with your hand encouraging your dog to lift his paws on to the surface - give reward

Caution – If you encourage your dog to jump up on you he may do the same to other people thinking this is OK

Pray

Your dog puts his front paws on your bed with his nose down until you say Amen

- Say 'Sit'
- Say 'Paws Up'
- Hold the reward between your dog's paws so his nose is between his paws
- Say 'Pray'
- Say Amen then give him his reward

Caution – small dogs might now be able to reach the bed so let them pray on a cushion or foot stool

Got a Headache

Your dog lies down and puts a paw over his eyes

- Say 'Down'
- Hold reward under your dog's paw. He will lift his paw to get the reward say 'Got a Headache' and reward
- Say 'Wave' and 'Got a Headache' to encourage your dog to lift his paw higher
- Jackpot

Got a Migraine

Your dog lies down and puts both paws over his eyes

- Say 'Down'
- Say 'Got a Headache'
- Hold reward under the paw that is on the ground (his other paw should be covering his eye)
- Say 'Got a Migraine' your dog should lift his other paw to get the reward
- Again encourage your dog to lift his paw higher and higher so that he covers the other eye
- Jackpot

Caution – Dogs with very short legs may have difficulty with these tricks

Come

Your dog returns to you and sits. Your dog needs to be hungry to highly toy motivated

- Start in an enclosed or fenced area
- Allow your dog to wander away
- Say your dog's name
- When your dog looks at you say 'Come' while showing him the reward
- Lure him into the 'Sit' and reward
- If he doesn't come call his name happily and excitedly then run away from him
- If he doesn't come walk slowly towards him and lure him with a reward until he takes one step toward you, lure him into a 'Sit' and reward him
- Walk away from your dog and repeat from the beginning
- Gradually increase distance until your dog comes to you every time

Caution – Use a 30 foot line when practicing without a fence

Dance

Your dog stands on his hind legs and walks or hops in a circle

- Say 'Look at me'
- Say 'Stand'
- Hold reward high above your dog's head and say 'Take it'. As your dog lift his front legs off the ground give him the reward
- Repeat, gradually increasing the height of the reward until your dog stands on his hind legs
- Repeat and as your dog stands on his hind legs move the reward in a circle above your dog's head
- Your dog will move around following the reward
- Say 'Dance' and give reward
- Repeat saying 'Dance' holding the reward up high and as he goes on his hind legs again move the reward around in a circle getting your dog to follow and reward

Caution – Larger or overweight dogs may have difficulty with this trick. Little dogs often do this trick without training

Sit – Stay

Once told to stay your dog will remain in the chosen position until told to come

- Say 'Look at Me'
- Say 'Sit'
- ⌘ Say 'Stay' count to 20 seconds and give reward
- Repeat saying 'Stay' and swivel around in front of your dog and repeat the command 'Stay'
- Count 5 seconds – give reward
- Repeat again take one step away from your dog and tell him 'Stay'
- Once your dog can 'Sit – Stay' for 20 seconds, start moving further and further away and for longer periods of time (when training outside use a 30ft leash for this)

Down – Stay

- Say 'Look at Me'
- Say 'Down'
- Repeat instructions from ⌘ above

Stand – Stay

- Say 'Look at Me'
- Say 'Stand'
- Repeat instructions from ⌘ above

This way

Your dog walks on a loose leash and stays within 30' of you

- Attach a 30' leash to your dog's collar
- Allow your dog to sniff and wander, within the 30' length, while you are walking
- As your dog nears the end of the 30' leash call loudly 'This way'
- Step on the leash if your dog does not turn to follow you
- A few sessions like this will train your dog to stay within 30' of you

Food on Paw

Your dog will lie with reward on his Paw until given the command to 'Take it'

- Say 'Look at Me'
- Say 'Down'
- Say 'Stay'
- Place reward on floor in front of your dog
- Say 'Wait
- Say 'Take it' and let your dog take the reward
- If your dog moves before the 'Take it' command quickly pick up the reward and start again
- Once you have several seconds between the 'Wait' and 'Take it' commands repeat gradually moving the reward closer until the reward is on your dog's paw

Food on Nose

Your dog balances reward on his nose and then once you give the release command he throws it up and catches it

- Say 'Look at me'
- Say 'Sit'
- Pet your dog's head with 2 hands. Bring your hands forward along the side of your dog's muzzle – your thumbs are holding a reward on the top of his nose
- Say 'Wait'
- As you remove your hands say 'Take it'
- Repeat gradually removing any pressure from your dog's nose, making usre that you do not remove your hands completely until your dog is still for at least half a second
- Your dog will eventually be able to catch the reward from his nose when you say 'Take it'
- Gradually increase the time between 'Wait' and 'Take it'

Caution – Flat faced dogs may not be able to manage this trick. Also dogs with very narrow noses may have problems

Play Dead

Your dog lies down on his side with his head of the floor

- Say 'Look at Me'
- Say 'Down'
- Say 'Stay'
- All of your dog's legs must be on the same side as his nose
- Holding reward in your hand lure your dog's ahead to the floor
- Say 'Play Dead' and give reward
- Repeat just saying 'Play Dead' luring his head down with the reward
- Say 'Play Dead' gradually moving further away from the luring position until you are eventually saying 'Play Dead' from a standing position and your dog will lie down and 'Play Dead'
- Jackpot

Alternate commands can be 'Bang your Dead' or 'I've got a gun I'm going to shoot'

Keep close – Slow, Jog, Running

Your dog walks by your side keeping pace with you

- Say 'Look at Me'
- Say 'Sit'
- Show your dog the reward – put it in your left hand and hold your hand down by your side
- Walk away from your dog say 'Keep Close', as soon as he gets to your left side in the 'Keep Close' position give him the reward
- Slowly increase the time between when your dog has to walk by your side in the 'Keep Close' position and giving him the reward
- When your dg is walking close to you, occasionally stop and lure your dog into a 'Sit' position with the reward. If you do this every time, your dog will learn to automatically 'Sit' whenever you stop
- Once your dog has mastered 'Keep Close' walking, try jogging and running

Caution – for small breeds use tongs or a wooden spoon with peanut butter enabling the reward to be close to their nose.

Spin

Your dog spins to the right in a circle

- Say 'Look at Me'
- Say 'Stand'
- Hold reward 1" from dog's nose
- Using the reward as a nose magnet move your hand in a clockwise allowing your dog to follow
- When the dog returns to stand position say 'Spin' and give reward
- Gradually increase the speed of your hand making your dog 'Spin' faster
- Give reward saying 'Spin'
- You dog will eventually 'Spin' on command
- Jackpot

Twirl

Your dog spins to the left in a circle

- The same as 'Spin' only counter-clockwise
- Jackpot

Most dogs will have a preference to either spin or twirl

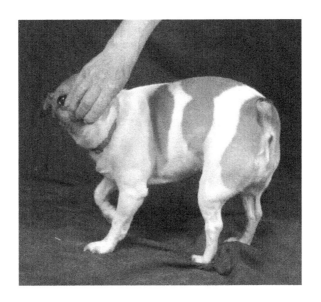

About Turn

While walking your dog in a 'Keep Close' position both you and your dog turn 180 degrees and carry on walking in the opposite direction

- Start walking with a reward in your left hand, using it as a nose magnet to keep you dog close
- Say 'About Turn' and slowly walk in a semi-circle to the eight until you are walking in the opposite direction
- Slowly reduce the size of the semi-circle to the right until you are pivoting around with your dag following you
- Once your dog is doing 'About Turn' to the right, start doing it to the left beginning with the larger semi-circle

Caution – for small breeds use tongs to hold reward in front of their nose

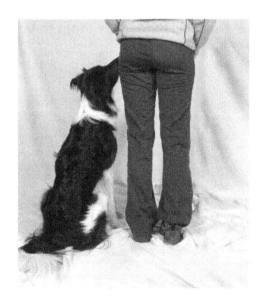

Pivot Right

From a sit position your dog follows as you pivot to the right and sits by your side

- Say 'Look at Me'
- Say 'Sit' making sure your dog is on your left side facing forward
- Use reward as nose magnet as you slowly turn to the right in a very tight circle
- Sure your dog into the 'Sit' position
- Jackpot

Pivot Left

From a sit position on your left side, your dog will turn to the left with you and resume a sit position

- Say 'Look at Me'
- Say 'Sit'
- Place you left foot in front of your dog at a 90 degree angle
- Your left leg should be touching your dog's face forcing his hose to point in the same direction as your left toes
- Bring your right foot alongside your left foot
- Say 'Pivot'
- Your dog will turn to the left with you, say 'Sit'
- If your dog does not follow you once you have turned left, take one step forward then say 'Sit'
- Jackpot

Heel Up

Your dog sits facing you. Your dog then walks around your, and assumes a sit position on your left side facing forward

- Say '<u>Come</u>'
- Say '<u>Sit</u>'
- Hold reward in your right hand
- Using the reward as a nose magnet lure your dog around your back saying 'Heel Up' transfer the reward into your left hand behind your back as your dog follows
- As your dog comes around to your left side lure your dog into the 'Sit' position and give him his reward
- Jackpot

1.

2.

Rear View

3.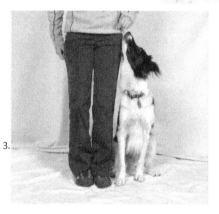

Finish

Your dog sits facing you. Your dog then walks to your left side, turns 360 degrees and assumes a sit position facing forward on your left side

- Say 'Come'
- Say 'Sit'
- Holding a reward in your left hand use it as a nose magnet to lure your dog to walk in a circle in your left side slightly behind you
- Once he has completed the circle bring him forward so that his toes are pointing in the same direction as your toes, lure him into a 'Sit' position
- Say 'Finish' and reward
- Jackpot

Go to Bed

Your dog will walk over to a designated area, lie down and stay there

- Put leash on your dog
- Say '<u>Look at Me</u>'
- Say 'Go to Bed' while pointing to your dog's sleeping area
- Hold leash and walk your dog to his bed. Say '<u>Down</u>' then say '<u>Stay</u>' giving the hand signal
- Reward your dog
- Repeat until your dog starts to walk over to his bed himself – reward
- Once your dog is going to his bed and lying down increase the time before giving his reward. Your dog should be happy to stay there for half an hour or more

Catch

Your dog catches an object on command

- Toss small pieces of food reward towards your dog's mouth
- Say 'Catch' as he catches the food
- Toss a soft toy towards your dog's mouth say 'Catch' and reward when he catches it

Fetch

Your dog will retrieve thrown items for you

- Toss a toy in front of your dog say '<u>Catch</u>'
- Exchange the toy for a reward and say 'Fetch'
- Repeat encouraging your dog to return to you with the toy saying 'Fetch' in exchange for a reward

Drop it

Your dog will drop whatever he is holding in his mouth

- Toss a toy in front of your dog
- Say 'Fetch'
- When your dogs returns to you with the toy, show your dog a reward in your hand and say 'Drop It' and exchange the toy for the reward
- Repeat and praise lavishly

Kiss

Your dog licks your cheek on command

- Put something tasty on your cheek (peanut butter or cheese wiz)
- Say '<u>Look at Me</u>'
- Offer your cheek to your dog and say 'Kiss' as he starts licking your cheek
- Offer your cheek with smaller and smaller amounts of tasty treat until there is none
- Reward your dog after he kisses you on command (once you are not using treat on your cheek)

Find the Ball

Your dog finds the hidden ball

- Play ball by dropping the ball in front of your dog
- Say 'Find the Ball'
- When your dog gets the ball make a big fuss and give reward
- Start tossing the ball further and further away until your dog finds the ball every time
- Next, show the ball to your dog, then place it in a slightly hidden place letting your dog see where you are putting it, but not able to actually see the ball
- Say 'Find the Ball'
- If your dog cannot find it, encourage him to the correct direction by tapping the ball
- When your dog finds the ball make a big fuss and give him a reward
- Gradually hide the ball in harder places for him to find and say 'Find the Ball'
- Each time he finds the ball in a new location make a big fuss and give him a reward

Find the Keys

Your dog will locate hidden keys. Your keys must have a non-metallic tab for your dog to pick up

- Gently toss the keys in front of your dog
- When your dogs looks at the keys, reward and praise him lavishly
- Continue tossing the keys saying '<u>Fetch</u>'
- When your dog goes to the keys and picks them up say 'Find the Keys' and encourage him to bring them to you
- Exchange the keys for rewards and praise
- Start tossing the keys in different directions and locations saying 'Find the Keys'. Always reward your dog with a treat when he returns the keys to you
- Hide the keys while your dog is watching you – say 'Find the Keys'
- Encourage and assist your dog by patting the hiding place if he seems confused
- Continue hiding the keys in different locations. Always make sure that the keys can be reached by your dog
- Jackpot

Caution – small dogs may have trouble picking up the keys, especially a large bunch

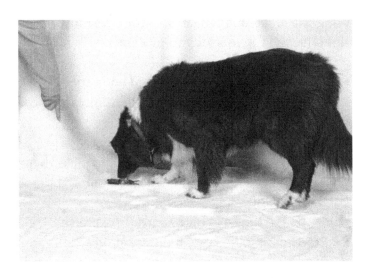

Find a Person

Your dog finds a person hidden out of sight

- One person with a reward hides from you and your dog
- You say to your dog 'Find _____ (insert name)
- The person hiding calls your dog until he finds them – then gives reward
- Continue practicing until your dog finds the other person on the command 'Find _____(name) without the hidden person calling your dog

Crawl

Your dog will crawl forward from a down position

- Say '<u>Down</u>'
- Hold a reward just in front of your dog's nose on the floor
- Move reward **very slowly** along the floor
- Your dog will follow the reward
- Say 'Crawl' and reward your dog
- If your dog constantly gets up use a low coffee table so that your dog has to crawl under it to get his reward

Caution – very large or overweight dogs may have trouble with this trick

Ring the Bell

Your dog will 'Ring the Bell' to let you know he needs to go out

- Place the bell on a rope and attach it to the door knob
- Say '<u>Come</u>' to your dog
- Hold a reward behind the bell so that your dog touches the bell with his nose
- Say 'Ring the Bell' and reward
- Gradually hold the reward further and further away from the bell until your dog just rings the bell on command (his reward can also be opening the door to let him out)

Caution – Some dogs will ring the bell incessantly in order to get a reward

Speak

Your dog barks when asked to 'Speak'

- Say '<u>Look at Me</u>'
- Create a situation where your dog will bark (knock on the door, jump up and down, make barking noises etc...)
- Say 'Speak' also give hand signals as shown on page 72 and give reward

Shhh

A wonderful command that stops your dog barking

- When your dog is barking (3 or more times in quick succession) offer a food reward but do not release it from your hand
- While your dog is sniffing the food he will not bark. Say 'Shhh' give reward
- Repeat adding 2 seconds each time between your dog not barking and giving the reward

Caution – Dogs that bark excessively do not need to be taught 'Speak' *only* **'Shhh'. Naturally silent dogs may have difficulty learning 'Speak'**

Whisper

Your dog makes low soft sounds on command. This is easier to teach once your dog knows 'Speak'

- Say 'Look at Me'
- Encourage your dog to vocalize by giving the command 'Speak' but don't reward until the bark softens a little, Say 'Whisper' and reward
- Practice 'Speak' and 'Whisper' so that your dog understands the difference using the hand signals
- Sometimes a high pitched singing voice will start dogs vocalizing softly

Caution – your dog may constantly 'Whisper' with the hope of being rewarded

Speak

Whisper

Take Food from my Mouth

Your dog gently takes a reward from between your lips

- Say 'Look at Me'
- Say 'Gently'
- Put a large reward between your lips, with most of the reward outside your mouth
- Put hour mouth close to your dog's mouth and let him take the reward
- Use smaller and smaller rewards the more confident you get!

Caution – young puppies have needle sharp teeth and can be over enthusiastic. Older dogs and puppies can be restrained with a collar and leash until they learn to take the reward gently

Hold Food in Mouth

Your dog holds his reward half in/out of his mouth until you give the release word

- Say 'Look at Me'
- Say 'Sit'
- Use large reward when first teaching this trick
- Open your dog's mouth and place the reward in his mouth so that half is sticking out
- Hold your dog's mouth closed
- Say 'Hold It'
- Let go of your dog's mouth and say 'Take It' letting him eat the reward
- After doing this a few times try again without holding your dog's mouth
- Gradually increase by 1 second intervals between saying 'Hold it' and 'Take it'
- If your dogs takes the rewards before the 'Take it' grab his mouth and retrieve the reward and try again

Caution – Make sure your dog allows you to take food out of his mouth without biting you before you try this trick!

Wag your Tail

Your dog wags his tail on command

- Say 'Look at Me'
- Say 'Wag your Tail' in a really happy voice – praise your dog
- Your dog will wag his tail just because of your tone of voice

Caution – Dogs without tails will not be able to do this trick – BUT come can wag their rear ends

Shake your Body

Your dog shakes his body on command

- Start when your dog is wet
- Say 'Look at Me'
- Say 'Stand'
- Run your hand along your dog's back from his tail toward his head to ruffle his fur
- Your dog will shake to smooth his coat down
- Say 'Shake your Body'
- Use less and less eater and fur rubbing each time until he just shakes on command

Caution – stand in front of you dog or you will get soaked. Also please note that most dogs will only shake their bodies once and you will probably have to wait about half an hour to try again

Put your Toys Away

Your dog will pick up his toys and put them into a box (the box sides must be low enough that your dog can easily put his head over the edge)

- Stand by the box
- Toss a ball
- Say 'Fetch'
- As your dog brings the ball back to you, hold a reward over the box at the same level as your dog's nose
- When your dog drops the ball to sniff the reward the ball will drop into the box
- Say 'Put your toys away' and reward your dog
- Repeat with the ball several times then repeat with other toys
- Gradually decrease the distance of the toss until you are just pointing at the toys to be put in the box
- Start moving further and further away from the box a your dog becomes more accustomed to this command

Afterword

Thank you for reading this book and hope that you have enjoyed it. If you liked it a lot tell all your doggie friends and of you think it can be improved tell us!

Remember to have lots of fun while using this book and make sure your doggies pal is having a good time also. Lavish them with lots of praise and teats and don't forget their jackpots.

You have now "Tricked your dog into obedience". While having a wonderful time with your intelligent and willing canine partner you can amaze and astonish your friends and family with your skill.

The bond you create with your dog will be like no other. Unconditional love and loyalty once formed is a bond that will not be broken.

About the author

Nancy Milburn has been training dog for over 30 years, She had a training centre, free range boarding kennel and opened the first dog day care in Ontario. After using all the traditional methods of dog training she developed this innovated way of training which now has gone mainstream as positive reinforcement reward training

She has retired from full time dog training but is still involved with local rescue societies and occasionally give seminars and private lesions.

Nancy lives on an island in northern Canada with her husband and dogs.

https://www.facebook.com/nancy.milburn.33

Made in the USA
Monee, IL
01 August 2021